HADRI
WALL

Where have all the stones gone?

A QUEST

by Wendy Bond

With grateful thanks to Hadrian's Wall Community Champions

First printed November 2016

Design by Diane Ridley

Handwriting by Aidan Brachtvogel

Published by readme publishing ltd
11 Park Avenue, Haltwhistle, Northumberland NE49 9AT

ISBN 978-0-9956747-0-7

Foreword

Hadrian's Wall is not only a well-studied monument, but a much beloved one. People travel from around the world to view and examine the carefully managed remains that are on display, enhanced by the dramatic, rural scenery that Wall runs through. Locals regularly walk the many paths that parallel the Wall or navigate across its course. And when you visit the Wall, you can almost always find yourself engaging in pleasantries with locals and visitors from near-and-far!

However, what many visitors fail to appreciate is that the Wall is only one (if rather large) monument of the rich and vibrant history of England's northern border counties. Along the length of the Wall, many important historic monuments can be visited, for example Hexham Abbey (founded AD 674) or the twin foundations of Jarrow-Monkwearmouth, where the venerable Bede wrote his scholarly works in the 9th century AD. There are castles of various sizes, like Halton and Thirlwall, and parish churches, and more beautiful farmhouses, barns, and out-buildings than can be counted. All these buildings of course made use of the abundant stone of the region, but many also borrowed, stole, or recycled (depending on your perspective) from Hadrian's Wall.

So when you visit the Wall and look about you, and then think it's not as big as I thought it would be, then refer back to this book, and look about you again. Hadrian's Wall, even when you are not directly on the line of the Wall, is all around you. As Wendy shows us, it forms the very foundations of the communities found along its length!

Rob Collins, Newcastle University
Nov 2016

Contents

HADRIAN'S WALL

What happened to all that stone?

Those of us who live "on Hadrian's Wall" are, not surprisingly, very familiar with our own portion of the national monument. Whether we live in an estate in the city of Newcastle, in one of the small villages in Northumberland or Cumbria, or on one of the isolated farms balanced high above the valleys, we know our Wall's surfaces, its ups and downs, its associated earthworks. It may be only a couple of feet high where we live - or 8ft high - or simply a bump or discolouration in the grass - to us it is unmistakable.

However, for many of the thousands of visitors to our stretch of Hadrian's great works delineating the Frontiers of the Empire - all now designated as the World Heritage Site - especially those people who are much more familiar with fences or hedges as field dividers, the Wall can be hard to find, hard to distinguish and occasionally rather disappointing.

A child who has seen a copy of one of the brightly coloured books about what it was like in Roman times may well feel as if confronted with the Emperor's New Clothes - and might legitimately ask - "But where has it all gone?"

The Wall at Banks turret

As it happens, this is a very good question. And the story of what happened to those stones that once reared, high and imposing, a "monument to Rome's purposiveness", as J Collingwood Bruce[1] called it, across Northern Britain from coast to coast, is in fact our local history and, I think, worth the telling.

My next door neighbours to the north are at Thirlwall Castle and to the east they're at Carvoran fort,which perhaps explains why I have, over the decades, become interested in the fate of those stones and the people involved in that story. Obviously this will be an incomplete account - there's a lifetime's pottering round the area still to be done. But I have enjoyed trying to pull it together.

In the process, I have met some extraordinary people, and found a variety of attitudes to the Wall, too. You may enjoy meeting some of the people I have come across. I hope, too, you will contemplate some of the practical ways of enjoying a visit to the Wall that this tale might suggest.

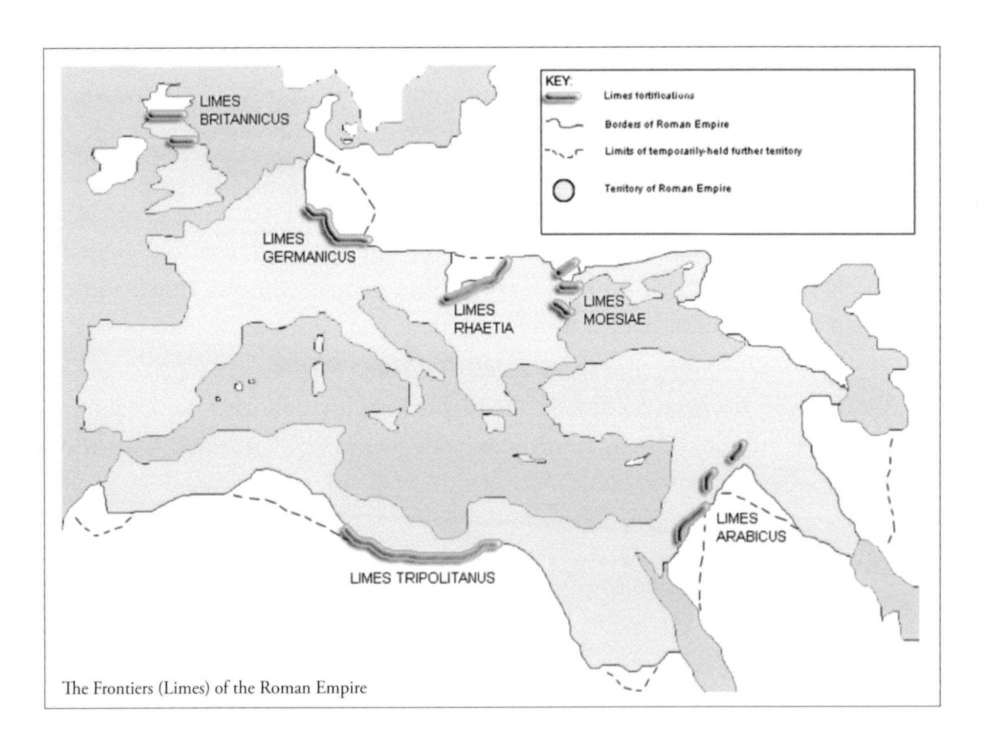

The Frontiers (Limes) of the Roman Empire

Chapter 1
WHERE THE STONE CAME FROM AND HOW THE WALL WAS MADE

It is worth first considering how much stone we are talking about. The sum is a challenging one - 80 miles or so, by about 2.5 metres wide by possibly 5 metres high, by whatever a cubic metre of stone weighs! One calculation comes up with 2 million cubic metres of stones, some of them rubble, but most of them carefully squared sandstone blocks.

Very important to realise, is how skilful the men of the Roman legions were in first cutting the stone and then laying it correctly. This was no haphazard business. They knew their stone - better in fact than almost all the people who came after them[2].

The locations of some of the quarries used by the Romans are known; often names carved on the rock face indicate who the men were who had been working there.

Inscribed quarry face at Fallowfield Fell
(P)ETRA FLAVI CARANTINI "the rock of Flavius Carantinus"

Sometimes the wedge-holes used to split the stone can still be seen on the rock face. Fewer than 50 quarries have been confirmed to retain evidence for Roman activity. The insights they provide into Roman technology mean they are all nationally important.

Irregular blocks of sandstone were usually dressed to shape at the quarry. The stones are generally similar in size and shape - ideal both for men to carry and for fitting together as facing stones on both sides of the Wall.

Holding it all together was lime mortar, made by burning the local limestone, also quarried nearby, as described by Pliny the Elder in Roman times, and as practised still in Romania today[3]. The lime produced was ground and mixed, dry, with sand and gravel. Only when it was about to be used as mortar was water added to the mixture, as it hardens very quickly. When a couple of courses of facing stones had been laid on the foundations and carefully pointed, a mass of fluid mortar was poured into the space between and irregular smaller stones were "puddled" into it. And so it grew, course by course, incredibly strong, and so wide that scaffolding was probably not needed.

As each unit of soldiers completed another 45-metre stretch of Wall, they carved their details on to a facing stone. We still have about 150 of these, mostly now in the museums to preserve them. These help scholars to build up a picture of how the work progressed and who was involved.

A centurial stone from Sewingshields
"The century of Gellius Philippus"

The Romans were introducing the concept of writing into the country, as well as that of building in courses of stonework, and straight lines! Security, meanwhile, was undertaken by the auxiliary solders, a less elite force than the legionaries.

It was the legions that built the Wall. A Roman legionary had to be as efficient a construction engineer as he was a warrior. All the various technical skills were covered. Ronald Embleton's lively painting (see frontispiece) of how the Wall might have been built gives a good impression of some of the tasks. These contemporary carvings on Trajan's column in Rome show typical legionaries at work. Neither of them gives much hint of what it was like to work on an unpacified frontier area with no civil administration, being interrupted by attacks from the peoples on both sides whose lives were clearly going to be totally disrupted by this barrier.

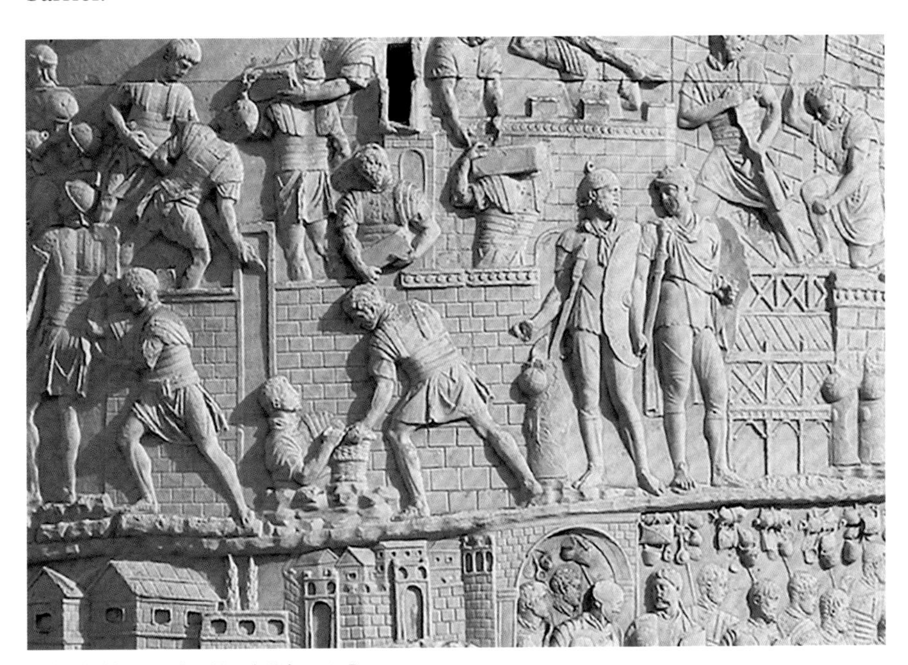
Soldier builders carved on Trajan's Column in Rome

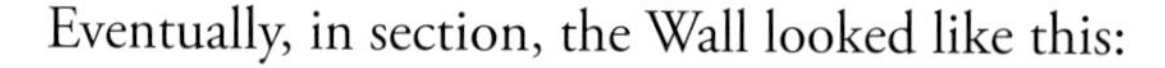

Eventually, in section, the Wall looked like this:

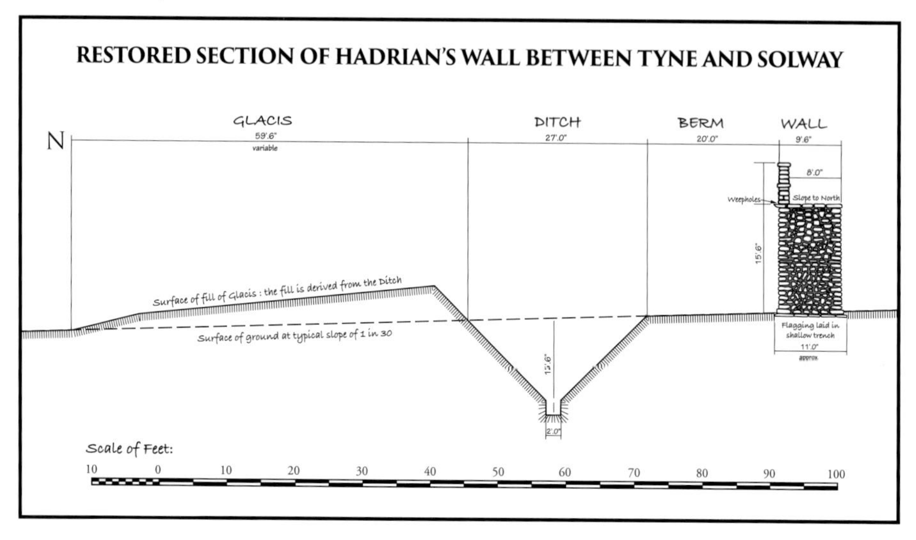

We know more. In 1972 the Government raised the school leaving age to 16, not entirely to the delight of many pupils at the time. One creative solution was to bring the new "top classes" from Gateshead schools to Vindolanda fort where they actually built a section of the Wall - discovering a huge amount by this experimental archaeology project[4]. For instance, they found that each stonemason needed 360 litres of water every day. And if you stand on the highest stretch of the Wall today, you will be hard put to see, in the glorious view spread before you, any easy way to source any water at all up there!! However, the Romans have always been experts in transporting water, though the aqueducts in Wall country are hard to trace as they wind along the contours for miles, shallow indentations in the earth rather than the splendid arched constructions in some Roman towns.

In addition to the Wall, of course, there were the regular turrets and milecastles, several splendid bridges across the various rivers and about 16 forts, and no trouble or expense was spared. Hadrian, on whose orders the whole edifice was constructed, had a reputation to keep up as "an emperor distinguished above all others for his ambition as an architect and his ruthless demands on the labour of his troops[1]". There was also the precious record in the inscriptions on tombstones and altars of the people and their history.

All in all, a colossal amount of stone was involved. Where is it now?
What happened over the next two thousand years?

Chapter 2
WHAT HAPPENED WHILE THE ROMANS WERE STILL AROUND

One thing is sure: however splendid the Wall and its forts might have looked when finally completed, before 137 AD when Hadrian died, they were not going to stay the same for long.

All too soon, under orders from the next emperor, Antoninus, the troops were sent north to build yet another frontier wall across the narrowest part of Scotland. Thereafter, there followed a century during which, in general terms, powerful men with units of a well-trained army at their disposal vied violently with each other throughout the Empire, in intensive rivalry to "wear the purple". In Britannia, the army was also repelling attacks by sea from Saxons and Scandinavians, from Scots and Picts by land. The Wall was breached - and repaired using local labour.

As a result, a Wall fort might have 1,000 men living there at one time - and be in the hands of a small garrison of 150 the next. The layout of the forts and the uses of the buildings within them changed countless times. Worse, sometimes the drains stopped working.

There is also the indisputable fact that all the walls ever erected, to keep people in or to keep them out, have proved irresistible to attack and destruction. Just as homo sapiens has always been on the move, ever since the first stone tool was chipped, whether for curiosity, greed or need.

At first, the Wall was usually manned by people from across the Empire, including Bulgarians, Syrians and Romanians - it was the safest way to keep newly-recruited and trained men loyal. The first British recruits would be sent to serve far away. By the third century, however, British-born sons were being absorbed into the army, first as a matter of course, later by decree; soldiers were allowed to marry their local women; towns grew up around those forts where the living was easy and in relatively peaceful times the forts became positively domesticated.

So when the army and administration were probably withdrawn in 409, it was in some cases natural that the obvious leaders among those who stayed behind should continue to control their men and to take food and service from the local people - in exchange for protecting them in times of trouble, in the strongest parts of the old forts.

The Roman roads remained extremely important for trade, and forts at a crossroads, like Birdoswald, were well placed economically at least for a while. In fact, the fort at Birdoswald was a highly defensible site, surrounded by the cliffs that rise above the great bend in the river to the south and the stone Wall to the north. Already, by the end of the fourth century, the ruins of the stone granary had become the base for a large wooden hall and it seems distinctly possible that a community could continue there. Imagine the ex-officer, now more resembling a chieftain, seated in his hall, attended by his men, a great fire burning at night in the hearth (a pair of Roman brooches have been found at the spot).

Reconstruction of the hall and service buildings of the second phase of post-Roman buildings at Birdoswald

It was not sustainable for long, of course, although Birdoswald might have been occupied until as late as 520. We have no written sources for what happened but, somehow, over the next two centuries, some of the successful war-lords and their bands agglomerated into, first, many small kingdoms and, eventually, two large ones.

There is a strong local tradition that the infant son of one of those left-behind Roman officers living in the neighbourhood was captured and carried off by Irish pirates. He grew up in Ireland, and became known as Patrick!

Chapter 3
THE NEXT SETTLERS AFTER THE ROMANS AND WHAT THEY MADE OF THE WALL

The Anglo-Saxons and Vikings who raided and infiltrated the Wall country over the next centuries were devotees of wood rather than stone, on the whole. On the east coast, Bede and his fellow monks speculated as to who had built the Wall and why, mostly very erroneously. They do not seem to have thought it had any relevance to them.

The Normans didn't arrive to settle as far north as the Wall until the reign of Henry ll (1133 - 89). King Stephen had handed Cumbria back to David of Scotland in exchange for support during the Anarchy. So this next group of stone-builders didn't arrive on the Wall scene until well into the twelfth century AD. This explains why there is nothing in the Domesday book about the Wall.

The Normans are of course famous world-wide as castle-builders, so it's not hard to see what would happen next. The first castle built from that handy pile of nicely shaped stones may have been Triermain, erected by Hubert de Vaux who obtained his barony near Gilsland from Henry in 1157.

> All that is left to see at Triermain is a set of earthworks and a solitary corner of the old gatehouse. Rather peculiarly, this tiny piece of gatehouse masonry still stands almost at its original height of over 9 metres!

The stones are nevertheless, sadly, immediately recognisable!

The first baron of Thirlwall's first, 12th-century, home above the river near Greenhead was wooden but in 1330 John de Thirlwall was granted permission to crenellate and forthwith made himself a 4-storey fortified house with walls between 2.5 and 3 metres thick with towers on top. The clue lies in that word, "river". Even though the name, Thirlwall means "break through the Wall", there must have been a Roman bridge there quite as fine as that at Willowford, to carry the Wall across the Tipalt Burn. Not a trace of the bridge remains, but an imposing amount of the castle is still standing, now the protected home of swifts and bats[5].

Thirlwall castle

You can see how easy it is to recognise the Roman stones in the picture!

A really nice thing to do, I found with the top class from Greenhead First School, is to get children to measure up a stone they have selected at that particularly good stretch of the Wall at Walltown Crags, then make a template of it in newspaper. They can then go off with this and find for themselves just where some of the stones have finished up - at the impressive buildings like Thirlwall Castle, but also just about everywhere, as this form of recycling went on till the middle of the 20th century, in the large and small buildings and farms that form our glorious heritage of vernacular Northumbrian architecture and field walls.

The other effect of the Normans was to recycle the Wall for churches, from the tiny, humble 12th-century church at Upper Denton to the mighty Lanercost Priory, founded in 1166.

Upper Denton church

Both contain a considerable amount of the stone from the Wall and from the fort at Birdoswald. The Chancel arch incongruously squeezed into Upper Denton church (sadly no longer in use) probably came from Birdoswald. The building stones certainly came from the Wall. Lanercost shows very clearly the local red sandstone used for the western end of the Wall.

Lanercost Priory

Possibly the smallest building using recycled Wall stones -
the "netty" on the line of the Wall at Sewingshields

Chapter 4
THE WILD TIMES WHEN THIS WAS LAWLESS LAND

A barony in the Border country became an increasingly inconvenient place to settle, as the ownership of the Borders counties swung to and fro, first between the English and the Scots, and then, when it became ungovernable, between the warring clans of Border folk. The Thirlwalls moved out.

For the next few centuries the area was known as the Debatable Lands and largely avoided by strangers. The clans, known and feared as Rievers, or Moss Troopers, lived by raiding, in defiance of the lords of the Marches sent to control them.

They built fortified houses called bastles, or pele towers.

These needed to be fireproof and strong to withstand a raid which usually involved stealing cattle from the byre on the ground floor of the building. A typical bastle house had walls four feet thick - with a ladder to the house door on the upper floor, to be drawn up at night and in times of trouble. Inevitably, more Wall stone was recycled.

The "Vicar's Pele" tower, Corbridge

Notable characters like Johnny Armstrong and Kinmont Willie feature in the ballads and legends of the time; the savagery and danger continued for three centuries until the Union of 1702.

The house door, reached by a ladder, at the rear of Glenwhelt farm today[6].
The initials indicate that a member of the Armstrong clan lived there

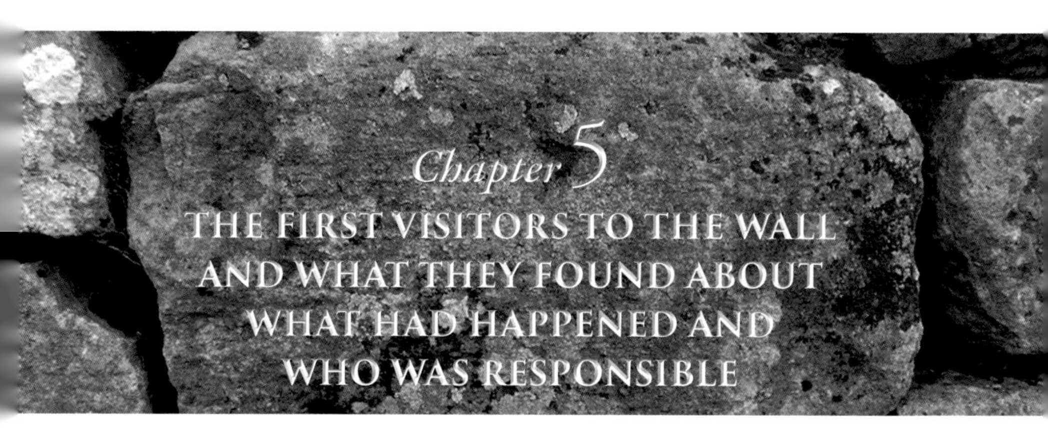

Chapter 5

THE FIRST VISITORS TO THE WALL AND WHAT THEY FOUND ABOUT WHAT HAD HAPPENED AND WHO WAS RESPONSIBLE

The Borders were rightly avoided for most of this time by all but a very few intrepid seekers after knowledge, of whom, the redoubtable and thorough historian, William Camden is a great example. He was determined to see as much as possible for himself and to record the history and state of the entire country.

Though understandably constantly worried about an attack from the brigands, he rode through Tynedale at the end of the 16th century in quest of the Wall, to make sure his great book, *Britannia*, was accurate. He found quite a lot of it standing.

> At Walltown: the wall thereby was both strongest and highest by farre: for scarce a furlong or two from [Carvoran], upon a good high hill, there remaineth as yet some of it to bee seene fifteene foot high and nine foote thicke, built on both sides with foure square ashler stone, although Bede reporteth it was not above twelve foot in hight

There is still one of the best stretches of the Wall here today, but definitely not 15 feet (5 metres) high.

Camden himself quotes John Fordon, a somewhat biased Scottish historian:

> The Scottes (saith hee) when by conquest they had gotten the possession of those Countries which are on this side the Wall toward Scotland, beganne to inhabite them; and having of a sodaine raised a sort of the Country people with their mattockes, pickaxes, rakes, three tined forkes and spades, made wide gappes and a number of holes in it, by which breaches they might passe in and out readilie at their pleasure.

So there is our first mechanism for the destruction of the Wall - the mattocks, pickaxes, etc used by the locals to breach the Wall to open it up for the Scots. In the absence of written sources, there is a common tendency in subsequent commentators to denigrate the local inhabitants of the area at this period about whom they knew next to nothing!.

Camden, like us, was looking for clues about what had happened to bring about the ruination of the Wall. At Corbridge he found more:

> there remaine still sundry reliques of antique worke, among which King John searched for ancient treasure, supposed to have beene buried there. But hee was overtaken with his owne vanity, and deceived of his great expectation no lesse than Nero when hee searched for the hidden wealth of Dido at Carthage. For nothing found hee but stones

A royal treasure seeker, as far north as this, is well worth adding to our list of villains!

Surely less reprehensible are the women that Camden found at Melkridge, by the river, beating their laundry on an old altar. They will not be the last examples of the local people making use of Roman stonework that takes their fancy! The same thing happens still, of course, all over the Mediterranean, where chunks of columns and carved stone are built into houses and field walls.

Another thoroughly likeable visitor to the Wall was William Hutton, the first man to walk the whole Wall, in 1801, at the age of 78, in a single pair of shoes and "scarcely made a hole in his stockings". He did all this in spite of his poor daughter's common sense pleas, and has left us a delightful account of the people he met as well as his research findings. I'd like to have met him.

In an isolated farm Hutton, too, found ancient stones in daily use:

> We arrive at Walltown, if a single house deserves the name. On each side the door stands a Roman altar, used for washing hands, kettles, dishes &c. and has at last the honour of supporting the dishcloth. I saw one old female, who treated me shily, and heard a younger, who durst not see me; and both, I have reason to think, wished me gone: but, perhaps I had the most reason to be frightened.

and at Housesteads:

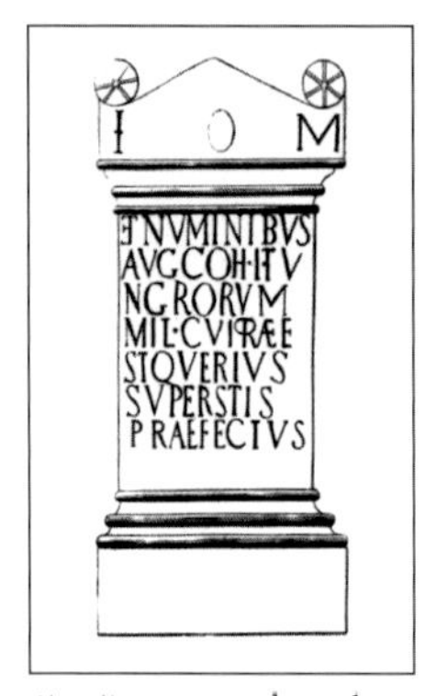

The altar once used as a door post near Housesteads fort

> In the farm house down in the valley, the jamb which supports the mantle tree is one solid stone, four feet high two broad and one thick, complete as in the day the workman left it

Hutton promised his readers to "enliven truth with a smile, with anecdote; and while I travel the long and dreary Wall, would have you travel with me, though by your fireside; would have you see, and feel, as I do, and make the journey influence your passions as mine are influenced." He was quite aware what people might think: "'What can exceed the folly of that man, at seventy-eight, walked six hundred miles to see a shattered Wall!'"

But his perspicacity failed in one thing: "Perhaps, I am the first man that ever travelled the whole length of this Wall, and probably the last that ever will attempt it" !

He walked all the way from Birmingham - and back, believing that "those who... chose to ride... could not be minute observers". Very true, and surely endorsed by our National Trail walkers today.

Hutton was passionately angry when he discovered how vulnerable the Wall was. It was a period of unusual, settled peace and the new century's new ideas inspired everyone to build! We admire eighteenth-century buildings and many splendid examples shot up in the North. Hutton was unimpressed by any of this nonsense.

At Castlesteads (picture on p42), towards the western end of the Wall near Walton, a brand new house and formal garden had completely replaced the fort of Camboglanna on the high bluff overlooking a bend in the river Irthing, a couple of years before Hutton arrived. He was furious:

> Other Stations preserve the ruins, but this only the name; and is the first which has been sacrificed to modern taste.

William Hutton was not one to pass by in despair if he could do something about it, either.

> At St Oswald's, the road turns a little to the left, for a few yards, and leaves the Wall to the right; but very soon crosses it again.
>
> Had I been some months sooner, I should have been favoured with a noble treat; but now that treat was miserably soured.
>
> At the twentieth milestone, I should have seen a piece of [the] Wall seven feet and a half high, and two hundred and 24 yards long: a sight not to be found in the whole line. But the proprietor, Henry Tulip, Esq. is now taking it down, to erect a farm-house with the materials. Ninety five yards are already destroyed, and the stones fit for building removed. Then we come to thirteen yards which are standing, and overgrown on the top with brambles... this grand exhibition must be seen no more. How little we value what is daily under the eye!

Feel the fury!

> ... I desired the servant with whom I conversed, 'to give my compliments to Mr Tulip, and request him to desist, or he would wound the whole body of Antiquaries. As he was putting an end to the most noble monument of Antiquity in the whole Island, they would feel every stroke. If the Wall was of no estimation, he must have a mean opinion of me, who would travel six hundred miles to see it; and if it was, he could never merit my thanks for destroying it

There is a local tradition that Henry Tulip Esq did desist from further depredations after this stern rebuke[7].

The appearance of this elderly traveller in his plain black clothes and green umbrella, carrying pen, ink-bottle and papers, alarmed many of the people he called on in these remote places and he often received a cold welcome.

> But as information was the grand point in view, I could not, for truth, give up my design; an expert angler will play with his fish till he can catch him. With patience, with my small stock of rhetoric, and above all, the simplicity of my pursuit, which was a powerful argument, we became extremely friendly; so that the family was not only unwilling to let me go, but obliged

> me to promise a visit on my return. They gave me their best; they wished it better; I had been, it seems, taken for a person employed by the Government to examine private property for the advancement of taxation.

That could have been today! Few withstood his gentle, warm personality. Beds were hard to come by, and sometimes full of "the dancing gentry of the night". The Twice Brewed Inn had prepared a pudding about as big as a peck measure and a piece of beef out of the copper, perhaps equal to half a calf" for the gang of carters expected; another remote public house had no food or drink to offer him but milk "which was excellent; but they treated me with something preferable: Civility."

"Fifteen carriers,,, each with a one-horse cart …sat down to the pudding and beef …Every piece went down as if there was no barricade in the throat … They convinced me that 'eating was the chief end of man'"

This new phenomenon, the Antiquarians invoked by Hutton - remarkably tender-hearted according to him, in that Age of Reason! - brought a new invasion of the Wall countryside, in the next phase of our story.

Chapter 6
THE AGE OF THE ANTIQUARIANS - TO THE RESCUE? OR NOT?

New enthusiasm for the Wall and the achievements of the Romans went hand in hand with the changes in society that destroyed it. Miles of drystone walls were built of Wall stone as the enclosures movement spread, this land-grab reaching the Wall area later than the rest of the kingdom.

Walter Scott had surely recorded in his early second novel, Guy Mannering, some of his own thrill upon seeing the Roman Wall as a raw young lawyer in 1797, in the exuberant words of his youthful hero:

> 'And this, then, is the Roman Wall,' he said, scrambling up to a height which commanded the course of that celebrated work of antiquity: 'What a people! whose labours, even at this extremity of their empire, comprehended such space and were executed upon a scale of such grandeur! In future ages, when the science of war shall have changed, how few traces will exist of the labours of Vauban and Coehorn, while this wonderful people's remains will even then continue to interest and astonish posterity!' Having thus moralized, he remembered that he was hungry, and pursued his walk to a small public- house...

Richard Hingley in *Hadrian's Wall - a Life*, has described the growing passion and intrepid travels of the new breed of scholar and the link that they made with the Enlightenment's admiration for Ancient Rome as a model for Great Britain. Suddenly there were Societies of Antiquarians meeting in all the large cities[8], and setting out to explore.

This is what happened when they came up here:

Peace, through the Union with Scotland, had brought, even to the northern Wall country, the new ideas and ambitions of the Agricultural Revolution.

One farming family living on the site of a Wall fort now called Carvoran, the Carricks, were already long survivors in the Debatable Lands in spite of the perils of the reign of the Rievers. They took to agriculture seriously on land which Camden in 1599 and Robert Scott in 1702 described as full of great ruins and the remains of not just buildings but streets. This is Embleton's suggestion for what Carvoran looked like in its Roman heyday.

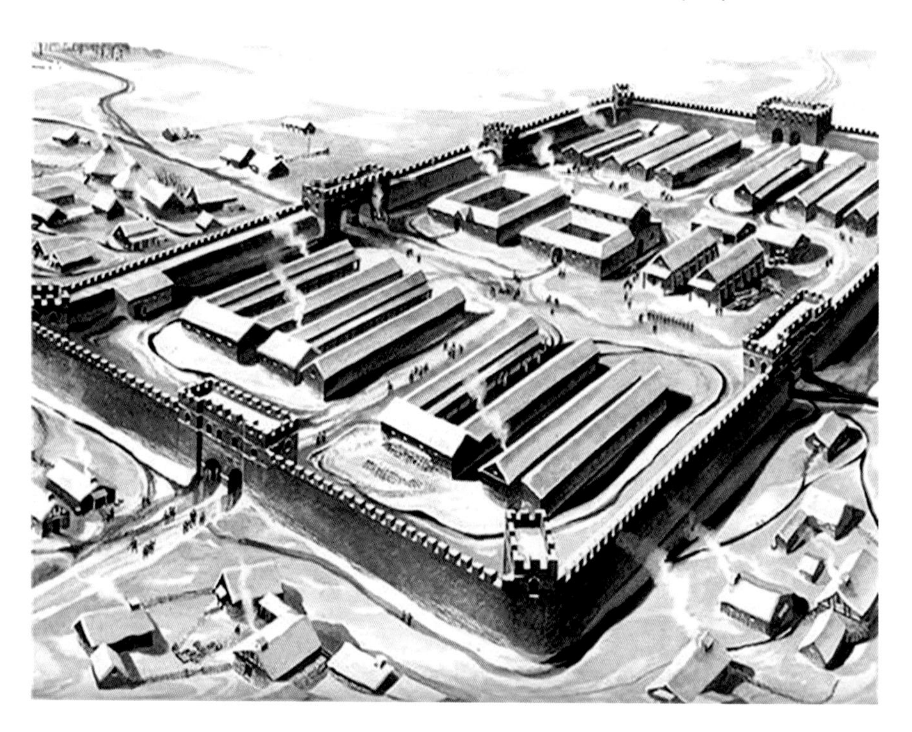

Camden saw:

> the groundwork of a castle of the Romans in forme four square, every side whereof taketh an hundred and forty paces. The very foundations likewise of houses and tracks of streets appeare still most evidently to the beholders

It was hardly going to be straightforward to make a living out of farming that, and it would be very costly in ploughshares! Undaunted, and like many others at that time in similar situations, the Carrick menfolk set about clearing the land for the plough.

What was different, however, about the Carricks was that, when the antiquarians found their way to the site, the family recognised and seized the opportunity for an early form of our current hope for hill farmers - diversification!

The normal local reaction, then as now, as Hutton had found and as Robin Birley has put it, to "those in formal attire" - was "resentment and suspicion".

I like to imagine the first John Carrick, about to pound yet another altar to smithereens when a stranger entered his yard. Pausing just long enough with his hammer in the air, he made the discovery that there was real money to be made from selling stones and artefacts to the visitors!

Thenceforth, for over a century, the Carrick family made a steady, non-taxable income from their finds as they cleared their fields, of great assistance in paying their feudal dues …

As a result, far more inscribed stones exist today from Carvoran fort than from any other Roman site in Britain - scattered far and wide, however. And there's no sign visible at all today of the fort that once housed 1000 men.

The very respectable Rev John Horsley FRS visited Carvoran several times between 1715 and 1730 :

> When I was last there, I purchased a Roman ring with a Victory on a cornelian, but coarse; as also a small altar lately found, with a very plain inscription upon it, dedicated by one Menius Dada, to the god Vitires.

Birley comments:

> At least the Carricks were prepared to rescue the bits and pieces from the plough …Most farmers did no such thing… [and so] there was a steady stream of respectable visitors to the Carrick front door.

This is Hodgson's curious encomium in the 1830s: (a hundred years after Horsley bought his ring!)

> The estate upon which Carvoran stands has for many generations belonged to the respectable family of the name of Carrick, who in draining and improving their ground, and especially in bringing the site of the station and its suburbs into

> a profitable state of bearing, have discovered and very laudably preserved a great variety of curious and valuable antiquities, many of which have from time to time been built up in the walls of their dwelling house and farm premises.

I'm not sure that dealing with the Carricks was necessarily all that easy! The next story doesn't change that impression - and does not have a very happy ending.

The current John Carrick, trying to get rid of a mound in one of his fields to the south west of the farmhouse, had unearthed a set of buildings. Hodgson described their excavation in 1830-31 by Captain Coulson, son of the Carricks' latest landlord. He found the remains of a bath house: its walls were "so strongly and beautifully painted that the colours glittered in the sun like stained glass. In the next year the altar of the Hamian Archers[9] was found standing on a pediment" .

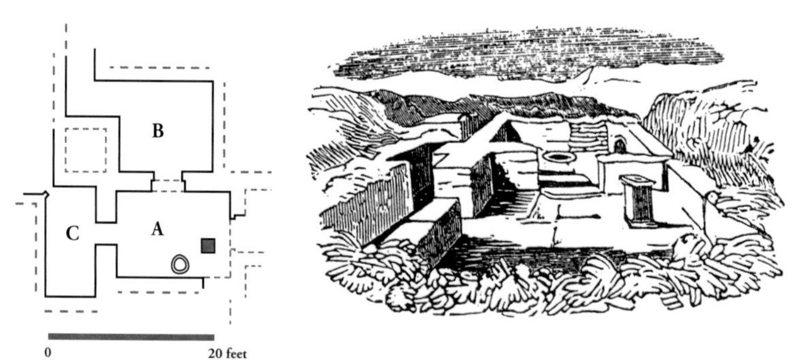

Plan of the baths, based on John Bell's version made in 1831, with a contemporary sketch[9]

It sounds wonderful. But:

> Mr Carrick, in self-defence against the trespass of the curious upon his fields, removed entirely the remains... and put the site of it under cultivation... Antiquities excite popular curiosity strongly, and to those remains the country people from far and near, in the fine summer Sundays, came in such numbers as to do great damage in treading down the crops of the adjoining fields

The altar of the Syrian Archers

I can add from personal experience one more instance of the disappearance of inscribed stones. My neighbour, some 40 years ago, was one of that particularly esteemed breed of quarrymen, the Shot Firers, - the men who, in all weathers, drilled the holes and inserted the explosive at the very top of the rock face at Walltown Quarry to bring down the whinstone, over the hundred years of the quarry's existence. Adam told me with a wicked chuckle, that, as they shifted the overburden, they had uncovered a huge stone, "9 feet across and covered with writing, and not in English..."

Pause. Sensation! Pause.

"We blew it up, of course - if them Antiquarians had heard tell of it they'd have closed the Quarry!"

Adam Potts, shot firer,
in Home Guard uniform

I was face to face with a radically different attitude to my surroundings, which needed to be explored. It brings me nicely to the quarrying of the Wall.

Some of the plant at Walltown Quarry, in the snow

Chapter 7
THE QUARRY WARS AND THE ARTICULATION OF THE VALUE OF A RUIN

Though the Wall itself is made of sandstone blocks, the rock it sits on, in the high, scenic central sector, is a ridge of very hard volcanic rock called the Whin Sill, formed during the massive movements of continents many hundreds of millions of years ago. It got the name because quarrymen in the north of England used the term 'sill' to describe a more or less horizontal body of rock and 'whin' for dark hard rocks.

Cut by skilled men into extremely hard-wearing blocks called sets, it paved the streets of most northern cities and the docks at Newcastle's Quayside. Chipped into small pieces it formed the basis of the tarmac surfacing the M6 and Newcastle Airport. As coal began to be worked out in the area, quarrying brought new investment and jobs.

The quarry at Walltown began in 1876, working eastwards from near Carvoran along the line of the Wall and destroying this turret even though the Wall had been scheduled as an ancient monument. There were no legal protections or sanctions in place at that stage.

The only surviving evidence for the Walltown turret demolished during quarrying

Then, in 1929, a Darlington engineer, John Frederick Wake, leased the mineral rights between the Wall and the vallum between milecastle 42 and turret 37A - the most spectacular stretch of the Whin Sill - with an entitlement to quarry within 10 feet of the Wall.

Fortunately, William Parker Brewis, who as a student had excavated at Corbridge before the first world war, got to hear about this. He campaigned vigorously in Whitehall and Westminster and then in the press, and a surprisingly large number of people, not just antiquarians and ramblers, pleaded on behalf of the ragged and really rather unprepossessing line of weed- & tree-covered stones on the scarp edge in this remote spot. What we see, stretches of neat stones, carefully rebuilt, conserved and made presentable, only appeared in the second half of the twentieth century.

Yet, In 1930, there was tremendous public support for some legislation that would prevent the destruction that Wake's lease could bring about, raised and carried on in the pages of the Times. Parker Brewis was tireless in campaigning, the archaeologists and scholars were heard in high places, and the threat was eventually averted. The detailed account of the battle can be found in Leach & Whitworth's excellent recent book, Saving the Wall.

The quarrymen of course felt very differently about the threat to their livelihood, however grim that livelihood was, and it really was grim! - as did the investors in the quarrying companies.

The quarry owners, and the landowners who collected rents from them, did not relinquish their rights and leases without a fight and compensation was required after the Ancient Monuments Act of 1931 finally brought legal protection for the Wall. But the public had shown how much they valued their heritage and there was no going back.

However, the bitter warfare between quarrymen, investors and antiquarians broke out again in the 1940s, complicated considerably by the fact that we were at War. There was demand for whinstone for aerodromes and Walltown Quarry advanced eastwards once more. The archaeologists acted behind the scenes, but in the press, local passions ran high.

27th August, 1943
TO THE EDITOR OF THE TIMES
Sir, — Why should we weep for Rome when the most splendid Roman monument in this country, Hadrian's Wall, is daily quarried for road metal?
Yours faithfully,
G.O. HOSKINS

Sept 7th 1943
Newcastle Journal & North Mail
Letters to the Editor
SIR, - The pother over the alleged damage to the Roman Wall, known as Hadrian's, gives an indication of the attitude of mind of many of our people. They revel in the past instead of concentrating on the future. I venture to say that these old relics are of little, if any, value. Like many other things of ancient times they should be scrapped, and if they were nothing but good would accrue.
A.J.

Sir, — In view of the great shortage of building material for houses for the living, may I suggest the whole of the ancient tyrants' wall be used for this purpose? Our forebears had the sense to do this, as can be seen in the farmhouses and other buildings in the neighbourhood of the Wall.
M.B.

... I discovered that this material quarried (not from the Wall) is being supplied to various Ministries for war purposes, and it would be interesting to know what some of the fighting men who are prisoners of war in Italy think about this controversy.
ENGINEER Newcastle

Sept 13th 1943
Newcastle Journal
Sir,—Are not some of your correspondents looking at the question of the Roman Wall from far too low a standpoint? A nation with a history such as ours must have much sentiment in its make- up. "Saxon and Norman and Dane are we" and our history goes back to the Romans and ancient Britons. We should cherish every link. If utility is to be our only guide why should we not pave the foot- walks with our parents' grave- stones and grow turnips on their graves - both "war efforts"?
....All over the world there are people interested in our unique relics on the line of the Wall and to destroy what is left would turn us in their eyes into uncultured barbarians.... the country round the line of the Wall is so majestic that our need should be great before we exploit it by turning it into a long-drawn-out quarry.
G. REAVELL

Sir,— ...To others who advocate vandalism I suggest that they arm themselves with a guide book and tour the whole length of the Wall and its fortifications.

If their imagination remains unstirred by the grandest monument that exists in England to the might of our Roman colonisers, if they would still destroy this wonderful work that has withstood the ravages of time for some eighteen hundred years, then they are indeed to be pitied, for they know not the value of these things.
J.N. CARR

... The glory of the Roman Wall is as false as Mussolini's Empire now in rags and tatters. I am prepared to substantiate my arguments with lantern slides and concrete facts. Meanwhile, let them go on quarrying, unless this farcical antiquity is of more importance than roads and R.A F. flare-paths.
THE VAGABOND

24TH November, 1943
NORTH MAIL

Town's need of Wall Quarries

SIR, —The letter signed by the chairmen of the Northumberland County Council and the Bridges and Roads committee regarding the Wall Quarry gives a very inconsiderate point of view. Are these gentlemen aware that, for eight years, these quarries and a small factory ... provided almost the sum total of employment for the manhood of Haltwhistle and district?

True, they did not absorb a great percentage of the available labour, but they did prevent the unemployed man-power figures from rising from 60 per cent to possibly 90 per cent...

3rd January, 1944
NEWCASTLE JOURNAL

HAULIERS' PROTEST

Sir, — ...the quarries have striven to produce in record time the essential road material for the building of several R.A.F. stations, and to that end the hauliers, working under many crippling restrictions have strained every nerve to keep their vehicles in a fit condition to cope with work of such national importance...

Incidentally, there are boys in the Forces who look to the quarries and the hauliers for the means of sustenance when they return to civil life.

December 9th 1944
NORTH MAIL

... If whinstone is of such rarity and value that this particular outcrop of it must be quarried, then surely it is better to shed our few silent tears over the spoiliation of what is both a glorious bit of England and a relic of the Roman occupation, and leave it at that. But let us make very sure that\this sort of thing is not repeated.
The whole of the remainder of the Wall, and particularly that part of it between the necks of Thirlwell and the North Tyne, should henceforth be preserved inviolate as an ancient monument.
... Let a fund be raised for the purpose, to which I would willingly subscribe.

The quarrying at Walltown thereafter went deeper and south rather than further along the course of the Wall; compensation was found for the quarry owners; men returned from the forces, relieving their womenfolk who had turned up for work in their place - it was a very close-knit community - and gradually the work ceased. Today the site at Walltown has a very different purpose. The Quarry at Cawfields, "now happily bought out by the nation"[11] stopped abruptly just before Milecastle 42.

My neighbour's widow remembered the day when her man came home to announce: "You know them Nine Nicks of Thirlwall? Well, there's eight now - we blew one up today!"

A Quarrymen's Supper in full swing

The vivid accounts of the Quarry by the men who worked there, and their widows and daughters - for many quarrymen died early, and horribly, from the dust - have been collected, thirty years after the quarry closed in 1976, through a series of "Quarrymen's Suppers" held in the Greenhead village hall. These form a treasured cultural archive. Told with hilarity and sparing no detail - you could not survive the conditions at the quarry without a truly wicked sense of humour - they add further spice to the after-life story of the Wall across the same few hundred yards already noted for the Carrick family's exploits, and in similar hard-bitten pragmatic vein!

Chapter 8
PUBLIC DESTRUCTION, PROTECTION, AND CONSOLIDATION

Far more devastating for the Wall, even than the effects of the quarrying, was the construction of what is commonly known as General Wade's Military Road, though Wade himself was long dead by the time the road was even begun. But it was his idea.

For, when Bonny Prince Charlie was advancing down the west coast route into England (in 1745) and making fast for Carlisle, the General and the forces of the Crown were based in Newcastle. They hastened westwards and three days later had reached Hexham in a sorry state. The snow didn't help; there was no road. The general went back to the city where the local landowners were spending the winter, and made his views clear - they should do what everyone else had already done elsewhere in the country and construct a toll road from Newcastle to Carlisle: with coaches thus able to travel they would soon recoup their costs.

The local grandees were unanimous - No one would ever want to travel along such a desolate route, they would never get their money back, etc etc.

In the end, our Military Road was the first road since Roman times built by public money, after an act of Parliament had been passed.

In the House, the men on the spot were able to point out a useful economy - there was a lot of stone, laid out in a straight line, already in place, perfect to use for the road's foundation. In vain did a solitary antiquarian, William Stukeley, plead against this act of vandalism and suggest the alternative of using the Stanegate route or the Romans' Military Way.

All this explains why the ditch can be seen so close to the B6318 road for mile upon mile in the east. And why the road west from Birdoswald is so very straight.

This was not the last time when the priorities of road makers overrode antiquity. Among other instances, as late as 1927, road straightening at the Newcastle end destroyed yet more of the remaining Wall.

Remarkably, when the railway was built in the early19th century, by accident or design, aside from once slicing through the Wall itself just by Gilsland Station, there was only a single "near miss": the Poltross Burn milecastle.

I wondered whether this was pure good luck, but Simpson and Gibson in their report on the excavations they carried out in 1909 state:

> The existence of this milecastle has been known since the days of Horsley, but, even in his time, the surface indications were not very evident, and its chief distinction was its name "The King's Stables" which it seems to have got in medieval times.

That intriguing name, "The King's Stables", lingering into the early 19th century and attached to slightly visible remains, may well have saved this important part of the monument at least. Poltross Burn Milecastle was safely excavated by the two archaeologists in the early years of the last century, as the trains passed alongside from the station 50 yards away.

Sections of the Wall began to come into the Guardianship of the Secretary of State from May 1933. Ten, of which six were gifted, were acquired in the years up to the end of 1939. Twenty-one more were taken on between 1945 and 1977, including one purchase and one more gift.

This meant, of course, a serious look at the Monument, hitherto the exclusive province of dedicated archaeologists and antiquarians. Nature and the elements had not been kind.

Traces of the Wall at Brunton

William Hutton had recorded at one spot :

> I was shown a large ash tree, which grew upon the very Wall, recently blown up by the root, and now rears up like a rounded pancake, eight feet high, and has drawn after it a ton of stones from the Wall still clinging and interwoven with the root.

In the 1930s the Ministry of Works shouldered the task of uncovering, rescuing and consolidating Hadrian's Wall. The archaeologists, Simpson, Richmond, Birley & Co, had finally established unquestionably that the edifice was indeed Hadrian's - putting to rest all the previous confusing claims of Agricola and Severus. Wall, ditch and vallum were now recognised together as one concept.

As sites came, one by one, into guardianship, the work began, often with one or two men, a horse and a cart: clearing away all the accumulation of earth, trees and hedges, then dismantling the stones, washing and numbering each one with yellow chalk, and re-laying them in the correct order. Tools supplied by the ministry were picks, spades and wheelbarrows. The mortar was mixed by hand. A site would be finished with turf and fencing where appropriate.

Outstanding among the small band of men actually doing this work was Charles Anderson[12] who became the devoted foreman, working for four decades on the project, apart from war service during which he managed to see Roman ruins in Algeria, Tunis and Italy. Thanks to Charles Anderson's hundreds of detailed photographs and notes, we can know exactly how each stage of the work was done and recognise the massive amount of physical effort that went on. What we see now and what these men were faced with are very different indeed!

By the 1970s, when I watched one man at work, a cement mixer had been provided. Recently I met a proud grandson of one Raffie Benson of Haltwhistle, a man known to have "pointed the stones on Hadrian's Wall"

The eighteenth-century mansion, Castlesteads, that completely replaced the fort of Camboglanna near Walton (see p. 20)

Chapter 9
CONCLUSION

So we are remarkably fortunate that we have as much of the Wall available to us today as we do, after 2000 years of wilful or accidental attack and neglect!

The story illustrates, too, that we can never sit back and assume that all will continue to be fine. Since the Wall area was designated as part of the Roman Frontier World Heritage Site, with all the conservation, access and community responsibilities that that status imposes on a country, there have been continuous downward lurches in the funding available for looking after this precious heritage. Climate change, too, has already produced pressures. We are delighted to welcome our visitors, but they do bring challenges.

What this story does tell us, though, is that we must continue the work of all those champions of the Wall in the past - and we must cherish, too, the people who live here and are ultimately its best guardians.

We can account in some measure for those missing miles of military construction: we can drive along on top of much of the Wall; we can locate it in local buildings; we can trace the gaps and ponder the work of past generatiuons; and we can identify the vigorous & pragmatic character of the local inhabitants who, having to survive along the line of the Wall through pretty harsh times, over eighteen centuries, have recycled it.

And we've met some of the people who have come to champion the Wall. William Stukeley, makes a plea for our own times too, as the frackers limber up:

> "In the times of the perfection of this work, it must [have been] looked upon as the best planted spot in the island; and we may imagine the glorious show of towns, cities, castles, temples & the like. This tribute at least we owe them, they deserve it at our hands, to preserve their remains."

NOTES

1 In the classic guide to Hadrian's Wall, often updated, Handbook to the Roman Wall, first published in 1863. My copy is the 12th edition, much updated by Sir Ian Richmond in 1965.

2 Will Higgs told me "The Wall is almost entirely constructed from sandstone. It was carefully chosen, where possible from local quarries, by people who knew how to choose stone, as demonstrated by its survival, not just the architecture, but the individual stones - you never see Wall facing stone crumbling.

"They also knew how to lay the stones the right way up, as they were in the quarry, and not with the grain vertical as you sometimes see in Victorian walls, making it more vulnerable to erosion as well as not looking right."

3 A fascinating EU-funded transnational LEADER project in 2002 brought together lime burners from Romania and architects and builders using traditional skills in the North Pennines, to compare different techniques and share knowledge, in both places. Our stone lime kilns can be seen throughout the Wall area, mostly as ruins.

4 We also learnt how effective the ditch was - you simply can't run down the slope of the ditch without looking down and therefore cannot avoid missiles thrown from above. My children loved doing this! In the three decades since then we've learnt how such a structure decays in the weather.

5 Northumberland National Park's 2000-2 project to consolidate the castle ruins, making them safer for adventurous children, also carefully preserved the nesting sites for the swifts that visit every summer and the bats that roost in the stonework during the winter. The bats are monitored by local bat groups. The lichen on the stones is directly descended from that growing there in Roman times.

6 The bastle was converted by the Armstrongs into a coaching inn in the 18th century when the Military Road arrived. Its new frontage vividly illustrates how much things had changed in 200 years. For the 16th-century inhabitants, the ladder gave protection. The later doorway is not only considerably more decorative, it incorporates the symbol of an early fire insurance society! (see p. 46)

7 According to Leach & Whitworth in their book, *Saving the Wall*

8 The Society of Antiquaries of Newcastle upon Tyne was formed in 1813, the oldest outside London, which may explain why so many of the Wall antiquities have survived compared with those from other Roman sites in Britain.

9 Jeremy Paterson told me, "The Syrian Archers came from the city of Hama on the Orontes. The city was the site of a terrible massacre of Sunnis by Assad's father in 1982 and has been at the heart of the destruction in the civil war today.

"There is a tombstone of one of the Syrian Archers in the Great North Museum. It is a bit battered, but you can see the two essential features: they had conical helmets and their composite bow has a distinctive double curve."

At Whistle Art Stop in Haltwhistle we painted a caravan for a family in the Calais camp with pictures of Hadrian's Wall and the Syrian Archers there.

10 John Bell was a noted surveyor and antiquarian. The plan was found in the Ashmolean Museum by Sir Ian Richmond.

11 Sir Ian Richmond in the Handbook. 1965

12 Alan Whitworth has written, "In recognition of the work that Charles Anderson carried out over nearly four decades on the Wall, with his work force of 26 masons and labourers, he was awarded the British Empire Medal in 1968 and the Imperial Service Medal in 1974. He was also made an honorary member of the Newcastle Society of Antiquaries of Newcastle upon Tyne in 1969. On 28 September 1969 an article was published in *The Sunday Express* on his work on the Wall, in which Anderson is quoted:

'The more I do it the more fascinated I become and the more I admire the Romans for their sheer engineering ability. I don't think many of the things we are putting up today will be standing in the year 3800. There is a compulsion about the job in which you discover new things every day and it spreads to every man involved. I have chaps who have been with me since before the war and who wouldn't dream of leaving until they have retired.'

Anderson's pet Alsatian dog was, naturally enough, called Hadrian.

Anderson understood the everyday life of farmers along the Wall and would take the time to talk to them regarding their concerns about the poor profits in agriculture, the problems caused by the ignorance of visitors, the effects of the weather and suchlike before dealing with issues like access to the site and the disposal of spoil from the excavations. The farmers in the area came to trust and respect him and he was a friend to many with whom he came into contact. He recognised that some farmers disliked 'the men from the Ministry' and went out of his way to re-assure them and to explain what he was trying to do to preserve the Monument. This invaluable ability to win their respect made a huge difference to the smooth running of the consolidation of the Wall."

Decorative eighteenth century front door at Glenwhelt coaching inn

Bibliography

Birley, R. *The Fort at the Rock: Magna & Carvoran on Hadrian's Wall,* 1998 Roman Army Museum Publications

Breeze, D.J. and Dobson, B. *Hadrian's Wall,* 1976 Allen Lane

Collingwood Bruce, J. revised Richmond, Sir I. *Handbook to the Roman Wall,* 1966 Harold Hill & Son

Hingley, R, *Hadrian's Wall - A Life*

Hutton's Wall, a Facsimile from the 1813 second edition. Templer Books

Leach, S. and Whitworth, A. *Saving the Wall: The Conservation of Hadrian's Wall,* 1746 - 1987 2011 Amberley

Wilmott, T. *Birdoswald Roman Fort: 1800 Years on Hadrian's Wall,* 2001 Tempus

List of Illustrations